I Can Be Wholly Devoted to God

He alone is your God, the only one who is worthy of your praise,
the one who has done these mighty miracles that you have seen
with your own eyes.

DEUTERONOMY 10:21 NLT

At the unveiling of the city's newest skyscraper, crowds gathered to celebrate the feat of architecture and engineering, commerce and creativity. Sunlight poured onto the observation deck as a city official cut the yellow dedication ribbon. Behind him were some of the many construction workers, designers, and engineers whose imagination, insight, and expertise contributed to making mere drawings a reality.

Only one expert—the architect—can truly take credit for the building's inception. One architect conceived of the shape, size, and details of the building. He intimately knows the building: inside and out. But everyone reaches for the spotlight. The architect is lost in the noise and clamor for glory.

You know this architect. He is your designer: the one responsible for your soaring heights and multitude of blessings. *He alone is your God.* Have you singled him out for glory? *The only one who is worthy of your praise.* Have you heralded to him a song of thanksgiving? The mighty miracles of your life are his careful design, plain for all to see. By faith, you can be wholly devoted to God, the architect of the strong, graceful, beautiful tower that is *you*.

Write down all the things you are thankful for in your life. Do you see God's hand of blessing in the big and little things? How can you offer all of yourself back to him today?

This journal belongs to

_____

Write down your
plans and God
will direct your steps

FAITH
DEVOTIONAL
JOURNAL

BELLE
CITY
GIFTS

Belle City Gifts
Racine, Wisconsin, USA

Belle City Gifts is an imprint of BroadStreet Publishing Group LLC.
Broadstreetpublishing.com

Write Down Your Plans and God Will Direct Your Steps

ISBN 978-1-4245-5084-5

Devotional entries composed by Shannon Lindsay and Michelle Winger.

Design by Chris Garborg | www.garborgdesign.com
Editorial services by Michelle Winger | www.literallyprecise.com

Printed in China.

15 16 17 18 19 20 21   7 6 5 4 3 2 1

Within your heart you can
make plans for your future,
but the Lord chooses the
steps you take to get there.

PROVERBS 16:9 TPT

Introduction

What you believe is the foundation of who you are. Be encouraged to go deep in your relationship with God as you reflect on the expressions of truth declared in these devotions. Journaling space gives you the opportunity to write down your thoughts and plans while trusting God with the details of your life.

God wants what is best for you. Consult him with your plans, trust his guidance, and allow him to lead you. You can depend on him; his faithfulness stretches to the skies!.

BY FAITH
I Believe I Am Accepted

If you confess with your mouth that Jesus is Lord and believe in your heart that God raised him from the dead, you will be saved. For with the heart one believes and is justified, and with the mouth one confesses and is saved.

ROMANS 10:9-10 ESV

How can it be that a humble prayer, a simple and yet astounding desire to lay down one's life and take up a life like Jesus Christ, establishes our eternity in the kingdom of heaven? Is it possible that such an act can really guarantee salvation? Our acceptance into God's family begins with this one act, yet it can feel too simplistic, too easy. We live in a world where, more often than not, we get what we deserve and nothing comes easy.

Sometimes, because we can't believe that acceptance can come from such a simple act, we reconstruct the gospel. We want to feel like we deserve God's grace, or that we have earned it, or that we've traded fairly. We build another set of requirements: more praying, more giving, more reading, more serving. Quiet time. Worship team. Children's ministry. Bible study. All of these habits are good and Christ-like, but they don't guarantee *more acceptance*. Not from God, anyway.

Paul emphasized how simple the path to salvation really is in his letter to the Roman church: if you believe it, say it. There is no other way. By faith, believe that your simple and earnest prayer assures your acceptance. And it is this simple. God's Word promises that it is.

Do you find it difficult to believe in the simplicity of God's requirement for acceptance? Reflect on the extra things you might be doing to try to gain his approval.

I Anticipate That God's Plans for Me Are Good

For I know the plans I have for you, declares the LORD,
plans for welfare and not for evil,
to give you a future and a hope.

JEREMIAH 29:11 ESV

There are two types of people in the world: those who can pack their bags at a moment's notice and take a last-minute vacation to Paris, and those who need months of planning and organization. You may be willing to do either one—it is a trip to Paris, after all!—but under which conditions would you most enjoy yourself? Could you trust that it would be everything you would've planned for yourself if you didn't thoroughly prepare it?

What if a well-travelled Parisian had personally chosen every hotel, restaurant, and attraction based on your individual tastes? Would you relax, knowing that the trip would be exciting yet safe, surprising yet tailored, unexpected yet promising?

When we consider our future, it can be difficult to trust that things will work out the way we desire. If only we could know that the plans for our future are certain! Consider that God knows the future, he knows you, and he knows exactly what you need. Read those words carefully… he knows exactly what you *need*. Not necessarily what you want, or desire, but what you *need*.

If you stick to the guidebook, your life might be just fine. You'll be a happy tourist in this world. But if you trust God, the one who knows you and your destination perfectly, you will see the secret places and hidden gems known only to the one who created them. Have faith. He has a plan that will take you places you never could have imagined. There is no better way!

Can you believe that God has the best plan in mind for your life? Tell him all the things you think you need, and then watch as he shows you what's best.

BY FAITH
I Know I Am a Child of God

All who are led by the Spirit of God are children of God. So you have not received a spirit that makes you fearful slaves. Instead, you received God's Spirit when he adopted you as his own children. Now we call him, "Abba, Father." For his Spirit joins with our spirit to affirm that we are God's children. And since we are his children, we are his heirs.

ROMANS 8:14-17 NLT

God is a good Father! He loves you with a love that is matchless and unwavering. Our earthly fathers have important jobs; primarily, they guide us to the love of our heavenly Father. Whether a devoted man's guidance models the Father's truly perfect and boundless love, or a flawed man's brokenness leads us to the Father's healing and compassionate love, both lead us home as children of God.

With lives submitted to Jesus Christ, we have the privilege of the Holy Spirit leading us in truth and in action. This Spirit, as Paul describes, is proof that we are adopted into God's family as children and heirs. By faith, we can take hold of our claim as God's precious and beloved daughters.

God teaches what true fatherhood looks like: loving authority, gentle guidance, unending grace, tender compassion, fierce protection, and perfect faithfulness. By faith, know that you are a child of God. Walk in the privileges of an heiress: full acceptance, spotless purity, humble confidence, eternal redemption, and an inheritance of life everlasting.

How has your earthly father shown you the immeasurable greatness of God's fatherhood—whether through a good or bad example? Thank the Lord for adopting you into his family and calling you his own.

BY FAITH
I Can Be Who God Made Me to Be

The fruit of the Spirit is love, joy, peace, patience, kindness, goodness,
faithfulness, gentleness, self-control; against such things there is no law.
GALATIANS 5:22-23 ESV

Making applesauce with autumn's abundant apple harvest is a beloved pastime across northern parts of America. Experts have developed award-winning recipes whose secret, they say, is combining multiple varieties of apples to produce a complex flavor profile. The result is a balance of the tart, sweet, crisp, mellow, and bold flavors for which apples are so well-loved. Each variety of apple is essential to the applesauce; their distinct flavors mesh into a delicious thing of beauty.

In the applesauce of God's ministry, each believer's spiritual fruit flavor-profile is essential. The fruit of the Spirit looks, tastes, feels, smells, and sounds different for each of us. In some, joy is a loud shout of excitement; in others it is quiet worship. One believer's kindness might feel soft while another's is firm. Peace can be expressed in as many ways as there are to use an apple.

When we compare the evidence of our fruit against other believers, however, lies are whispered to our flesh: *your fruit isn't as shiny, your fruit isn't as fragrant, your fruit is too mushy and flavorless.* A lie is born in thinking that all trees produce the same fruit. That just isn't true.

Your relationship with Jesus Christ is unique. He produces, between you and the Holy Spirit, an exceptional fruit that only grows from *your* branches. By faith, you can be who God made you to be. We are all capable and expected to grow fruit that exhibits the fruit of the Holy Spirit. When we come together, according to God's perfect recipe, for his glory, it is truly delicious.

In the past, how have you compared your fruit to others? Can you see how we are all made with a distinct flavor to benefit the whole of Christ's body?

BY FAITH
I Believe in the Authority
I Have as God's Child

The Spirit himself bears witness with our spirit that we are children
of God, and if children, then heirs—heirs of God and fellow heirs
with Christ, provided we suffer with him in order that we may also
be glorified with him.

ROMANS 8:16-17 ESV

In his amazing power, God appoints us to be ambassadors for his holy kingdom. Our job comes with humble authority and joyous expectations: we will suffer as Jesus did on earth to receive the glory that he does in heaven.

When we first lay our burdens at the cross, we inherit Jesus' authority to overcome sin and death. We can proclaim his name with all its power. When we continue to trust God, our faith is counted as righteousness, and we have the authority of God's new covenant—Jesus will return again to deliver us. As we walk out our faith, we proclaim the truth of the Gospel of Jesus with the same love that he showed to us when he died on the cross.

Our prayers, our worship, our hope, our faith, and all of our steps come under God's authority. With the power of the Holy Spirit, we have the authority and honor to suffer with Jesus so that we can be glorified with him. How can we use our authority to bring Jesus glory, even as we suffer for his name? As ambassadors, how can we foster a connection between Jesus and his lost sheep? Wherever we go, whatever we do, our God's name—and all its love, power, healing, compassion, and grace—goes with us. By faith, the authority you have as God's child is a testimony of salvation from sin and your inheritance of glory.

How does suffering play a part in your opportunity to bring glory to God? Ask
him for grace to walk through the suffering so you can also share in his glory.

BY FAITH
I Believe God Makes Me Beautiful

He has made everything beautiful in its time. He has also set eternity
in the human heart; yet no one can fathom what God has done from
beginning to end.
ECCLESIASTES 3:11 NIV

We've probably all heard an older gentleman declare that his wife is more beautiful now than the day they married. And we likely thought, *He needs glasses.* What we fail to recognize in our outward-focused, airbrushed society, is that time really does make things beautiful. More accurately, time gives us better perspective on the true definition of beauty.

Spending time with those we love affords us a glimpse into the depth of beauty that lies within. So while the external beauty may be fading, there is a wealth of beauty inside—and *that's* what the older gentleman was referring to.

God's Word says that he makes all things beautiful in his time. *All* things. Whatever situation you are facing right now, it has the potential to create beauty in you. Believe it! Perseverance, humility, grace, obedience—these are beautiful. But there's more. The beauty God creates in us cannot be fully described in human terms. There is eternal beauty to be found.

When we are met with challenges that cause us to run to God and sit in his
presence, we can't help but reflect the beauty of his character. What are you facing
right now that could be a catalyst for true beauty?

BY FAITH
I Know That What I Believe Is True

*Now faith is confidence in what we hope for
and assurance about what we do not see.*

HEBREWS 11:1 NIV

Where does belief originate? We can look to scientific evidence of the earth's creation by an intelligent designer, and there are many scientific specialists who can discuss the details passionately and convincingly. We can read the prophecies from Scripture that also point to the truth of God's power, presence, and passion. Then there are scholars, preachers, and authorities who tell you about the prophecies. The historic evidence of the existence of Jesus Christ comes with another set of experts who can explain the proof and compelling evidence.

Finally, we have his people: the humble followers of Jesus who have experienced his saving grace. We were blind, but now we can see. We were lost, and now we are found. We were dead in our sins, but now we are alive in Jesus Christ! This is all we can *know* for certain. We may not be scientists, theologians, or experts in apologetics, but we know that we were blind and God enlightened us. We were lost and God gave us a home. We were dead and he raised us from our graves and gave us hope. By faith, we know that what we believe is true.

God created the earth. He spoke the planets, oceans, and trees into being. He imparted to the prophets details of the coming Messiah, and Jesus came and fulfilled those promises in perfect detail. But our very testimonies—our transformation from death to life—are the simple and powerful proof that what we believe is true.

Take a moment to reflect on the undeniable truth that you are different today than you were before you knew God.

BY FAITH
I Will Walk in Boldness

Let us come boldly to the throne of our gracious God.
There we will receive his mercy, and we will find grace
to help us when we need it most.

HEBREWS 4:16 NLT

We have full access to the throne of God! Is there any throne on earth granting this much access, this little security, so much grace? Imagine walking into Buckingham Palace, unnoticed and unrestricted, without knocking or announcing yourself, and pulling up a chair alongside Her Majesty, the Queen of England.

"Hello, Your Majesty. Quite the weather we're having. I was wondering if you could give me some advice on a problem I've been having at home. Do you have some time?"

It's bizarre and ridiculous, obviously. There are procedures to follow, etiquette, protocol for seeing royalty—not to mention the armed guards, alarms, and jail, probably.

Thankfully, there is a royal throne toward which we can walk with boldness because we have all the credentials we need. There are no guards, no necessary payments, and no barred doors. Its occupant is the God of all creation, and he is eager to help us with anything we need. And his is the only throne that is worthy of our worship. Approach his throne, and shamelessly pull up a chair. He loves your company and will never send you away. By faith, walk in boldness as you approach the throne and lift your voice to him.

What do you need? Ask him without fear. What gifts has he given?
Thank him. What guidance are you looking for? His wisdom is yours if you will listen.

BY FAITH
I Choose Not To Be Fearful

Such love has no fear, because perfect love expels all fear. If we are afraid, it is for fear of punishment, and this shows that we have not fully experienced his perfect love.

1 JOHN 4:18 NLT

Fear rears its ugly head in lots of ugly ways; the spider waiting in your bathtub, the high bridge you pass going to your favorite park, the loud noise outside your bedroom window in the middle of the night. Fear can be gripping, paralyzing, or terrifying for some. For others, it is motivation to conquer weakness. Those fears are mostly related to phobias, which, one could argue, stem from basic human defense instincts. What about the fears that keep us awake at night? The worries and anxieties that cannot be brushed aside?

Jesus' followers had one such worry: what would happen on Judgment Day? Was Jesus' death enough to cover their sins completely and guarantee their eternity in heaven? John points out their fear as one of punishment. But there isn't room for fear alongside perfect love, and if we are abiding in the love of Jesus, then we have perfect love in us. Fear must surrender.

We must surrender as well. We must surrender to the truth that sets us free: Jesus died and is now alive—so our sin is dead and we are alive. *We are alive!* When the aisles of the grocery store fill with chocolate bunnies and plastic grass and colorful pastel eggs for listless shoppers pushing carts in silence, this truth should shake them from their stupor! *We are alive!* Death, sin, and fear are overcome! Jesus has overcome!

By Faith, you can choose not to be fearful, instead living with the resurrection in mind. Jesus has overcome it all; we have nothing to fear and no more debt to pay. Heights and spiders and enclosed spaces might still quicken your heart, but you can rest easy in his perfect love, now and for all eternity.

Are you alive with this truth? How can you train yourself to bask in the love of God? Fear cannot remain in the presence of perfect love.

BY FAITH
I Will Not Compromise

When troubles of any kind come your way, consider it an opportunity for great joy. For you know that when your faith is tested, your endurance has a chance to grow. So let it grow, for when your endurance is fully developed, you will be perfect and complete, needing nothing.

JAMES 1:2-4 NLT

The best products are built using the best ingredients. Some companies compromise, and when trouble inevitably comes, their products suffer and they lose money. But organizations dedicated to quality without compromise build things that endure. Oh, beloved, that our faith would be strengthened for endurance! What are we made of? Can we stand the test? Trouble is on the horizon, but we are advised to see it *as an opportunity for great joy.*

This isn't easy advice to follow, but in his wisdom, God gave his Word for our benefit. What would we expect him to say? *Dear children, when troubles of any kind come your way, curl up into a ball of despair for all hope is probably lost.* Of course not! God is building us to last! We would not gain blessing through hopelessness. No, he builds our faith with the highest-quality parts: hope in the promises of God's Word, humility from the grace that he has given us, and love for God who first loved us.

Built with quality, we can have *great joy.* Our endurance grows and we are proven *perfect and complete, needing nothing.* By faith, we will not compromise. We want more opportunities for great joy! Bring the tests! Grow our endurance! When the final product is revealed, we will shine like pure gold.

In what areas do you find it easiest to compromise? Ask God to help you endure through the testing so you will be found lacking nothing.

BY FAITH
I Will Find My Comfort in God

May our Lord Jesus Christ himself and God our Father,
who loved us and by his grace gave us eternal comfort
and a wonderful hope, comfort and strengthen you.

2 THESSALONIANS 2:16-17 NLT

There are so many things that we choose to comfort ourselves with: food, entertainment, relationships, music, or even just busyness… We'll choose anything to take our minds off the wave of emotion that is raging inside. It's much easier to grab a pint of chocolate ice cream, or throw ourselves into a project, than it is to face what's really going on. But those comforts just don't last.

The apostle Paul said that God is the God of *all* comfort (see 2 Corinthians 1:3). The things we use to comfort ourselves that aren't from God are destined to fail. They can't offer the hope, peace, security, or love found in the presence of God. They can't reach into the deepest places inside us and turn our sorrows into joy.

When you choose to find your comfort in God, you will not be disappointed. He knows everything you have faced since the moment you were born, and he knows the best way to comfort you right now.

How do you need to be comforted today? Will you choose to find it in God?

I Will Make Good on My Commitments

"The servant to whom he had entrusted the five bags of silver came forward with five more and said, 'Master, you gave me five bags of silver to invest, and I have earned five more.'
The master was full of praise. 'Well done, my good and faithful servant. You have been faithful in handling this small amount, so now I will give you many more responsibilities. Let's celebrate together!'"
MATTHEW 25:20-21 NLT

By committing our lives to serving Jesus Christ, we commit to investing the treasure he has given us and growing it to an even greater value for his kingdom. When our Master returns, we should have something to show for our years of serving him and proclaiming his name on earth. By faith, we make good on our commitment to Jesus by sharing the gospel, and serving widows, orphans, and refugees in our land. We love as Jesus loved.

We also commit to being faithful, honest, and diligent, just as he is. Our lives are a representation of Jesus, and our ability to make good on our commitments illustrates God's faithfulness. We are modeling godliness to a godless world. We demonstrate his truth, love, integrity, and mercy to a world lost in sin. By faith, we make good on our commitments to the world in order to shine the light of Jesus in the darkness.

Yes, we will make mistakes, and of course God's grace is sufficient for us. By faith, do what you say you will do; after all, God has kept his promises to you. Look forward to the day when you will hear the fulfilment of your commitment: "Well done, my good and faithful servant. Let's celebrate together!"

What do you find to be the hardest part of keeping your promises?
Spend some time reflecting on the faithfulness and dependability of God,
and let that be your motivation!

BY FAITH
I Will Walk Confidently

Be my rock of refuge, to which I can always go;
give the command to save me, for you are my rock and my fortress.
For you have been my hope, Sovereign LORD,
my confidence since my youth.

PSALM 71:3, 5 NIV

The foot traffic in the park was heavy: moms pushing strollers, joggers huffing over the trails, kids with baseball gloves and bats heading for open fields, couples meandering hand-in-hand under the leafy canopy. Observe closely and one can tell a lot about a person. Their posture, especially, is revealing. The man on the park bench, shoulders hunched, seems discouraged. One jogger lifts her head towards the sun, hopeful, while a mother's eyes dart nervously back and forth.

It is obvious when our hopes have sunk into shifting sand; we find no peace, no comfort, and no protective fortress from distress. Our foreheads wrinkle, our steps drift, our distraught hands clasp and wring. Our confidence is lost.

What do you see when you look in the mirror? Worry lines or laugh lines? Are your eyes cloudy with anxieties or bright with possibilities? Are you hesitant or confident? God is the rock on which you can firmly plant your hopes. By faith, lift your eyes to the Son and walk with confidence. The sovereign Lord is the only hope and assurance you need!

Write down the things that are distracting you from walking in confidence.
Give them to the Lord and watch him restore your hope.

I Know God Remains Constant in Change

*A furious squall came up, and the waves broke over the boat, so that it
was nearly swamped. Jesus was in the stern, sleeping on a cushion.
The disciples woke him and said to him,
"Teacher, don't you care if we drown?"
He got up, rebuked the wind and said to the waves, "Quiet! Be still!"
Then the wind died down and it was completely calm. He said to his
disciples, "Why are you so afraid? Do you still have no faith?"*

MARK 4:37-40 NIV

It takes time to adjust to changing situations. Sailors need time to get their
"sea legs," mountain climbers rest in order to adjust their lungs to altitude changes,
and scuba divers surface slowly to regulate pressure. Even adjusting to daylight-
savings can take some time.

During their time with Jesus in his ministry on earth, the disciples had to adjust
quickly to radical situations. A daughter was raised from the dead, a boy's meager
lunch multiplied to feed a crowd of 5,000, a demon was cast into a herd of pigs
that threw themselves off a cliff. Could they have woken up in the morning and
sufficiently prepared for such things? Then one day, they get in a boat and their
limited faith is tested.

It seems as though the disciples never really adjusted to the unpredictability
of life with Jesus. Have you? If they struggled while in his very presence, how can
we have faith to walk confidently into the unknown? We have his Word and the
assurance that his presence is all we need; he is constant in the face of change.

As his daughter, you are always in his presence. No matter what you are facing,
by faith, you can walk confidently. It may take some time, but he is prepared for
everything and will prepare you, too.

*What changes are you going through today that make you feel uneasy?
Can you trust that God is steady in the storm, and he will not leave you?*

I Will Find My Contentment in God

I have learned in whatever situation I am to be content. I know how to be
brought low, and I know how to abound. In any and every circumstance,
I have learned the secret of facing plenty and hunger, abundance and
need. I can do all things through him who strengthens me.

PHILIPPIANS 4:11-13, ESV

Paul shares with us his beautiful secret, which followers of Jesus Christ have been surviving on since it was penned, sealed, and delivered to the Church at Philippi. We are promised a life of persecution, sacrifice, and rejection. The key to unlocking contentment amidst the trials is in trusting that your needs have been met. Trust eliminates the spectrum between "life is good" and "life is bad." With trust, all life lived in the strength of Jesus is contentment. All life is satisfaction. Everything is a fulfillment of his promise that following him is every gift we need.

Contentment grows in the midst of growing discomfort. Joy is found despite the trouble we find around every corner. A life of faith prospers amid the ruins. By faith, find contentment in God. Comfort is found when you trust in your Father for everything. We don't need the trappings and the shimmer of the temporary. Whether we have everything or nothing, we trade it all for the eternal.

God strengthens us to endure these worldly wanderings for the hope and promise of our eternal existence.

What stops you from believing that God truly does meet your every need?
Can you believe him for contentment today? His ways are perfect and good.

I Trust God to Keep Me on the Right Path

Make me to know your ways, O LORD;
teach me your paths.
Good and upright is the LORD;
therefore he instructs sinners in the way.
He leads the humble in what is right,
and teaches the humble his way.
All the paths of the LORD are steadfast love and faithfulness,
for those who keep his covenant and his testimonies.
PSALM 25:4, 8-10 ESV

GPS has nothing on God. We use satellites because we want to know where we are going, how long it will take to get there, and how many miles we will travel on our journey. Our lives, however, don't have coordinates recognized by modern-day digital guides. Only our loving and faithful God leads us in the direction we really need to go. Not only that, but he teaches us his ways as we walk with him. He *instructs sinners* who humbly learn to be *good and upright*.

The world's guidance can instruct you to take a left—directly into a murky pond. Satellites aren't as accurate as God's perfect instructions. By keeping his covenant and testimonies, we stay on the right path.

With God, both the journey and the destination are worth the effort. We are transformed by travel; we are reinvented by a loving and faithful leader. When mapping out a travel itinerary, won't we look for a path of steadfast love and faithfulness? When we keep his covenant and his testimonies, we receive the promises he gives us in his Word. By faith, trust God to keep you on the right path.

Recall a time when you took a "wrong turn" in your life. Can you see God's faithfulness even in that moment? When you humble yourself and ask him for help, he is happy to guide you back to the right path.

BY FAITH
I Will Be Courageous

May he give you the power to accomplish all the good things
our faith prompts you to do.

2 THESSALONIANS 1:11 NLT

Courage is often associated with acts of bravery that defy typical human experience: running through flames to save a child, jumping in a raging river to pull someone to shore, or chasing down a thief to retrieve a stolen purse.

But courage doesn't always look so heroic. Courage is standing your ground when you feel like running; it's saying yes to something you feel God is telling you to do even when you aren't sure that you can do it.

Courage can be telling someone you don't want to hear their negative thoughts about other people. It can be sharing your testimony with a room full of people… or with one. Sometimes it takes courage just to leave your house.

When we place our trust and hope in God, he will give us the courage we need to do the tasks he wants us to do. If that includes doing something *heroic*, great! But let's not underestimate the importance of walking courageously in the small things as well.

What are you facing in your life right now that requires bravery?
Take the first step and believe that God will give you the courage to continue.

BY FAITH
I Know I Can Depend On God

Be strong and courageous. Do not be afraid or terrified...for the LORD
your God goes with you; he will never leave you nor forsake you.

DEUTERONOMY 31:6 NIV

Death and taxes. They say those are the two things we can depend on in
life. Of course they don't mention the neighbor who fails to return the cordless
drill (again), the empty fuel light blinking when you're late for work (again), and
the spontaneous yet cheerful visitor ringing the doorbell when you're still in your
pajamas at 3pm (again). Unpredictability is something else we can depend on!

Through every unpredictable situation, through all disappointments, delays,
and disruptions, we can cling even more confidently to the faithfulness of God. He
is the one solid rock on which we can firmly stand. He is steadfast and loyal, asking
us to trust in his promises. God commands that we not be afraid or terrified; if it
weren't possible, he wouldn't ask it of us. He guarantees that he will always be with
us, no matter where we go. If it weren't true, he wouldn't promise it.

Life will be shaky and unpredictable—*that* you can count on! But by the grace
of God you will never have to endure it alone. There is nothing that will cause
him to change his dependable ways. Death and taxes will come. So will life's
unpredictable twists and turns. But do not be afraid; God is by your side. By faith,
you can depend on him.

What things in your life seem dependable? Which seem unpredictable?
Trust that God will always be near you. He is the one you can cling to when all else
is shaking.

I Am Determined to Stay the Course

Do you not know that in a race all the runners run, but only one gets the prize? Run in such a way as to get the prize. Everyone who competes in the games goes into strict training. They do it to get a crown that will not last, but we do it to get a crown that will last forever.

1 CORINTHIANS 9:24-25 NIV

Runners are human beings that have honed the evasive skill of self-control. They have the willpower to overcome physical pain and exhaustion. They have the stamina to push past throbbing muscles, breathlessness, and lead feet. They have, first and foremost, the ability to follow through with the plan. Running may be on the schedule, but, like anyone else, runners have to actually put running shoes on and move their feet along the pavement. Sure, it's more comfortable on the couch. Yes, it's easier to walk, and many runners would rather get together with friends. But they have committed to the plan. And the plan says, *Get dressed, lace up your shoes, and get on the course. Now.*

So they do. This is the only difference between runners and non-runners. And it is the only difference between believers and non-believers. Believers in Jesus Christ have determined to stay the course because it's what is asked of us. Non-believers are also running through life, but their direction changes with the wind.

Running this race is the greatest challenge of your life. It requires self-control, motivation, and stamina. It requires submission to the training: saying yes every day to getting dressed, lacing up your shoes, and staying on the course. By faith, determine to run the race so that you will win!

What is hindering you from putting your running shoes on and hitting the track? Ask God to help you see life through his eyes, and let it motivate you to stay on course.

I Can Walk with My Head Held High

My thoughts are not your thoughts,
neither are your ways my ways, declares the LORD.
For as the heavens are higher than the earth,
so are my ways higher than your ways
and my thoughts than your thoughts.

ISAIAH 55:8-9 ESV

In times of war, army strategists benefit from high vantage points. Looking upon the battlefield from above is the best way to formulate strategies for their troops. Before the use of satellite equipment and heat-sensing radar, views were limited to ground level, forcing the use of maps and spies to predict enemy movement and position men. After their invention, hot-air balloons were used by generals in battle to accurately determine the locations of enemy troops.

In the same way, our lives benefit from a higher viewpoint. When we rise above our circumstances and see life, not from our own anxious, urgent, sometimes overwhelming perspective, but from God's, life's battles become less intimidating as eternity's promises rise into view.

God has plans for your life, but sometimes they are hard to see. The day-to-day defeats of life consume us and we struggle to confidently lift our head above the fray. When this happens, remember his high thoughts and ways, and believe that he will lead you. By faith, walk with your head held high, knowing that he sees everything that surrounds you. Trust him. He will lead you safely to the other side.

What decisions are you trying to make that require a higher vantage point?
Ask God for his perspective and let him lead you in his perfect way.

I Will Find Encouragement in God's Word

I wait for your deliverance, O Lord,
for your words thrill me like nothing else!
Invigorate my life so that I can praise you even more,
and may your truth be my strength!
PSALM 119:174-175 TPT

There is wonder to be found in snowflakes, raindrops, and even strange bugs. Though we often don't love the idea of encountering too many of those things, if we stop and look, if we allow ourselves to really *see* what is there, it's pretty amazing.

The same can be true of God's Word. It may be displayed in various forms and places throughout our homes, schools, work places, or church buildings, but if we don't stop to really drink in the words that are there, we can miss the rich blessing behind them.

When we believe that God wants to encourage us through his Word, we will no doubt find encouragement in it—because God intended it to be used for that purpose! Don't gloss over the beauty and depth of his Word. It's the only Word that carries the richness of eternity.

Where do you find your encouragement? By faith, believe that you will find it in God's Word today, and write it down when you do!

BY FAITH
I Can Endure Hardship

*Consider it pure joy… whenever you face trials of many kinds, because
you know that the testing of your faith produces perseverance. Let
perseverance finish its work so that you may be mature and complete,
not lacking anything.*

JAMES 1:2-4 NIV

Creating a diamond is, for the transforming coal, a long and painful process. Simple carbon undergoes an immense refining pressure that produces a wholly new creation. We might just see a cloudy rock at this stage, but there is another refining step to be taken. After the stone-cutter does his work, a precise shining diamond emerges: magnificent, glittering, brilliant.

When we endure hardship, the long and painful process can seem unfair. To the mother with terminal cancer, it seems excessive. To the abandoned wife, it seems unjust. To the orphaned daughter, it seems cruel. But our life stories are written by a compassionate Creator who is crafting a masterpiece. He is refining us, like the diamond, into something entirely beyond our imagination. And we can rejoice in the beauty he is creating. You may not see it now, but it's coming soon.

The pressure and the pain happen first. The coal cannot avoid this part. But it is the choice, after so much pain, to become more than clear rocks—to see our beauty and joy shimmering beneath the surface—and submit to the shaping and polishing of God's skilled and loving hands. Let the pressure not be for nothing. By faith, know that you can endure hardship and emerge stronger and brighter than ever.

What painful process are you enduring right now? Can you see the emerging beauty under the surface of the hardship?

BY FAITH
I Know Where I Will Spend Eternity

We are citizens of heaven, where the Lord Jesus Christ lives. And we
are eagerly waiting for him to return as our Savior. He will take our weak
mortal bodies and change them into glorious bodies like his own, using
the same power with which he will bring everything under his control.

PHILIPPIANS 3:20-21 NLT

The question of eternity is a heavy one; some choose to believe that death is the end of existence and the beginning of nothingness. Some believe in a heaven open to everyone, regardless of their life on earth, where we will all exist peacefully. Others believe in the existence of heaven and hell, but that only the most horrible people on earth end up in torment.

The Bible tells us the truth that heaven is a real place, inhabited by those who have accepted Jesus Christ as their Savior. Those who haven't trusted him will spend eternity alienated from him, which is the essence of hell: an eternity absent of anything good. But believers in Jesus' death and resurrection for the forgiveness of sins will live and share in his glory. Our bodies will be transformed and everything will come under his control.

What a relief to know the truth! Eternity is a guarantee, one way or the other, and yours can be one of heavenly citizenship. You have been promised an inheritance of glory, where all pain, suffering, and weakness will be transformed. All deception, hatred, and greed will come under the control of Jesus Christ as he makes all things new. By faith, your eternity is established.

How do you hope your eternity will be spent? What do you look forward to most about it?

I Choose to Lay Down My Expectations and Believe God for More

By Faith Abraham obeyed when he was called to go out to a place that he was to receive as an inheritance. And he went out, not knowing where he was going.

HEBREWS 11:8 ESV

Is it a surprise to learn that God can give you all that your heart desires and more? Is it a surprise to know that our human expectations are so limited that they cannot even begin to imagine the fullness of joy in Jesus Christ? We have expectations of glory, but God urges us to come up higher, to stretch our faith. Are we ready for more?

We have been given a very high calling and we cannot achieve it without some exercise. Like it or not, we must get a little uncomfortable, a little sore, a little sweaty. Maybe a lot. But we are capable of so much more than we know. We are braver than we believe. Stronger than we seem. Smarter than we think.

Believing God for more first requires commitment to the challenge; following God into the unknown is strenuous on both mind and strength, and without commitment we'll inevitably give up. It pushes the boundaries of faith, asking that we put aside our limited expectations and believe God's promise of joy. And just when we think we can't endure any more, God reveals the view from the mountaintop and all the strain is suddenly worth it.

We realize that the exercise itself is its own reward; the challenges are worth every drop of sweat and every moment of pain. With expectations stretched, faith is strengthened for God to use us in greater measure. We are ready for a higher climb to a greater height where we find more astonishing joy.

What do you want to believe God for more of? Can you stretch your expectations to believe him for even greater things?

BY FAITH
I Will Go Where God Leads Me

With weeping they shall come,
and with pleas for mercy I will lead them back,
I will make them walk by brooks of water,
in a straight path in which they shall not stumble,
for I am a father to Israel.

JEREMIAH 31:9 ESV

The journey of the believer is a lifelong pilgrimage that ends not at a religious temple or city, but in the kingdom of heaven. Our journey's hardships, sacrifices, and struggles are part of our displacement, and they won't end until eternity. Wherever the path leads, we follow. However long and dusty the road, we press on. No matter what storms lay ahead, we continue. With determined steps we press on toward our destination until we are welcomed home.

Before we began this pilgrimage, we were broken, dead in sin, and weeping from our wounds. Our merciful God redeemed us and brought us up out of the mire. It may not always seem like it, but this path he has set us on is full of restoration, nourishment, steadfastness, and love. The many steps of our pilgrimage are not walked alone, but alongside one who never gets lost, tired, or afraid.

He knows we were confused and alone for a long time, so he personally leads us. He knows we are thirsty, so there are sanctuaries along the way. He knows we were bruised and broken while stumbling along our old pathways, so he navigates a straight route for our safety. He is a good Father to us and we can trust his leadership. By faith, go wherever he leads, beloved. Your pilgrimage is a long and beautiful journey, and it's worth every step.

Where do you feel the Lord leading you in this season? Can you trust him enough to say you will follow him wherever he leads you?

BY FAITH
I Trust in the Faithfulness of God

Let us draw near to God with a sincere heart and with the full assurance that faith brings, having our hearts sprinkled to cleanse us from a guilty conscience and having our bodies washed with pure water. Let us hold unswervingly to the hope we profess, for he who promised is faithful.

HEBREWS 10:22-23 NIV

God is good and he knows all of your needs. He is faithful and he longs to show more of his glory and beauty. *God, show us more of you!* Show us how much you can do through our fellowship and communion. Show us how far your faithful hands can reach and how much love they will pour out upon your Bride. Prepare our hearts to say "yes" to your call. Clear a path and make a way so we can fulfill your plans.

We will not lose heart, God! By faith, we trust in your faithfulness. We love you fully, like children chasing after joy. Our love is pleasing to you, because you delight in your children. You sing over your children, notes and refrains here and there as we walk the earth, waiting for you. One day, your song will be complete, and when we hear its fullness, we will run to you!

Until that day, by faith, we trust in your faithfulness. *We hold unswervingly to the hope we profess* because we have *the full assurance that faith brings;* our hearts are cleansed and we are pure.

In what ways have you seen the faithfulness of God demonstrated in your life? Thank him for his sacrifice that has cleansed you and given you hope.

BY FAITH
I Believe That I Am Forgiven

"Her sins—and they are many—have been forgiven, so she has shown
me much love. But a person who is forgiven little shows only little love."
Then Jesus said to the woman, "Your sins are forgiven."

LUKE 7:47-48 NLT

It can be so hard to trust in complete forgiveness—so hard to trust that all of the horrible, shameful, repulsive sins of the past are known by Jesus and yet fully forgiven. If you were the repentant prostitute sitting at the feet of Jesus, would you believe?

Could you confidently listen to your sins, listed in detail for all to hear, and say, "Amen! I have been forgiven! Yes, even of that, hallelujah!" This woman's sins were known to all, and rather than hiding in shame away from the world, she sought Jesus because she believed in his forgiveness. He would not turn from her in disgust, shut her out, or reject her. By faith, she was completely accepted, loved, and redeemed.

The Pharisee's rebuke of her presence seems so heartless; doesn't he understand that no one could possibly have greater reason to rejoice than this woman? No offering of oil, poured out on the redeemer's feet, could be more pleasing than the one from these humble and grateful hands. Jesus loves the heights of her gratitude; they are equal to the depths from which she has been saved.

Can you relate to her burden? Can you relate to her pain and her shame?
Can you understand her deep and desperate longing to worship at Jesus' feet?
By faith, you are forgiven. Fully, completely, and lovingly. Share now, beloved,
in her unending worship.

BY FAITH
I Believe That God Is Good

*You are a chosen people. You are royal priests, a holy nation, God's very
own possession. As a result, you can show others the goodness of God,
for he called you out of the darkness into his wonderful light.*

1 PETER 2:9 NLT

God is good and he makes all things good. Evil is the absence of God's
goodness. Like light and darkness, goodness cannot exist in the same place as
evil. The world, however, often seems to exist in shades of gray. Light and darkness
tangle together to become something indecipherable and the resulting shadows
breed uncertainty.

Politicians, activists, and corporations love uncertainty because it encourages
a second look at what once seemed certain. What society believed was good has
shifted, but God never shifts. His goodness is certain.

Let's begin with that. *He is good.* Now, decipher the light from the darkness,
the good from the evil, knowing that God doesn't change and is always good. He is
good in unemployment, in sickness, in despair, in bankruptcy, in another's betrayal,
even when it seems like darkness is all around. *He called you out of the darkness
into his wonderful light.* You belong to him, you are chosen, and by faith, you can
believe in his goodness and walk in his wonderful light.

God is good and he redeemed you from your sin. He never leaves you. He has
reserved a place for you in his kingdom. He is light, and darkness cannot exist in the
light. By faith, believe that he is good.

List all the things about God that remind you of his goodness.
Thank him for choosing to share his goodness with you.

BY FAITH
I Know God's Grace Is Sufficient for Me

God is so rich in mercy, and he loved us so much, that even though we were dead because of our sins, he gave us life when he raised Christ from the dead. (It is only by God's grace that you have been saved!)... God saved you by his grace when you believed. And you can't take credit for this; it is a gift from God. Salvation is not a reward for the good things we have done, so none of us can boast about it.

EPHESIANS 2:4-5, 8-9 NLT

There is no greater education in the amazing grace of God than his own words. When the impact of his grace has saved you, these words have a particularly powerful and humbling effect. We have done nothing, yet we have everything. We were dead but now we have life. We didn't pay with money, flesh, or enslavement. We just believed.

Because of his amazing grace, and because we believe this truth, we have everything we need. Our eternity is established. Is there anything else we require? We have a salvation that cannot be lost, stolen, forfeited, or forgotten. And God's grace for us will never fail, fade, or diminish.

We cannot boast in our salvation, but we can sing praises from the rafters for this amazing gift. Sing long and loud, for grace is the one and only gift we will ever need. And we can share it, without losing an ounce of our portion. It multiplies over and over, as long as we are willing to give it away. By faith, know beyond a shadow of doubt that his grace is sufficient for you. It has been from the moment you believed!

Take some time to write your thanks to God for his undeserved gift of grace.

BY FAITH
I Choose to Be Grateful for All of Life's Blessings

Let your roots grow down into him, and let your lives be built on him.
Then your faith will grow strong in the truth you were taught,
and you will overflow with thankfulness.

COLOSSIANS 2:7 NLT

Gratitude makes a lovely countenance. When our cups overflow with gratitude, there isn't room for bitterness or criticism. Gratitude pushes away judgement and disdain and makes room for joy and grace. People walking in gratitude make very pleasant company. Their overflow of thankfulness blesses everyone, from families and friends to the people in line with them at the post office.

What a testimony to God's goodness! When we have an attitude of thanks, we confirm that we have been blessed. And beloved, we have indeed been greatly blessed. Beyond material blessings, beyond the blessing of health and home, beyond even the blessing of family and friends, we have the immeasurable blessing of faith. By faith, we build our lives on the Word of God. By faith, we grow strong and learn the truth of God. By faith, we *overflow with thankfulness.* Our thankfulness is a gift back to God.

Let your life be a testimony of gratitude. Let the aroma of your thankfulness touch the senses of everyone around you—a sweet perfume of God's faithfulness to you. He has blessed you and it is right that you would overflow with praise! Root yourself in God, build your life on him, and watch your faith strengthen.

Let your thankfulness overflow to the furthest reaches of your life, contagious and compelling, a countenance reflecting the glory of God. Tell him how thankful you are today!

BY FAITH
I Will Walk in Honesty

Truthful words stand the test of time,
but lies are soon exposed.
PROVERBS 12:19 NLT

Some people are terrible liars. Most children fall into this category. Their made-up stories and far-fetched excuses are sure to draw suspicion even in less-discerning adults. Sometimes we might even find their stories humorous or cute. The dog colored on the wall? Of course it did! The baby took the cookie off the kitchen counter and ate it? Sure thing.

But there's nothing funny or adorable about lying. Lies are destructive in every possible way. They can do long-lasting damage to our character and relationships. They destroy trust and stir up doubt. And they certainly don't bring us any closer to God.

Sometimes telling the truth is hard. Owning up to mistakes, bad decisions, and accidents doesn't come easily. In the end, though, the only thing a lie will do is make the situation worse. By faith, we can choose to walk in honesty. At least then we know that God will cover us.

A bad liar? That's something we should all strive to be. How can you make it a
point to walk honestly before God and others?

I Will Walk Honorably before God

The name of the Lord Jesus will be honored because of the way you live, and you will be honored along with him. This is all made possible because of the grace of our God and Lord, Jesus Christ.

2 THESSALONIANS 1:12 NLT

Honor awards are usually given to those who achieve excellence in specific fields. People are honored for their performance in musical, athletic, academic, and professional arenas. Some are honored for their exceptional bravery or intelligence. And rightly so. But if honor is given only for excellent achievement, how on earth can we be considered honorable with our less-than-impressive abilities?

The secret to living a life that honors God is found in depending heavily on his grace to cover us. By faith, we choose to walk honorably before him. We keep it simple. We do what we know is right, and we don't do what we know is wrong. We don't compromise. We don't chase after the shiny honor awards of the world. And when we get it wrong, we humbly admit our failure, accept God's forgiveness, and keep walking the narrow road.

It's crazy to think that we are even capable of bringing honor to God through our lives. We're so *human*, and he's so *perfect*. But that's precisely it—we aren't able to walk honorably on our own. We can't achieve the excellence standard required. It's only by his grace that we are considered worthy of his honor award.

Evaluate the honor awards you are seeking after right now. Will they ultimately bring honor to the Lord?

70

I Will Put My Hope in God

May the God of hope fill you with all joy and peace as you trust in him,
so that you may overflow with hope by the power of the Holy Spirit.
ROMANS 15:13 NIV

I hope it doesn't rain today. I hope I did well on that final. I hope he didn't forget our anniversary. I hope I get a promotion. Few things that we hope for contain the kind of satisfaction that lasts. Even if we get what we hoped for, what comes next? We have to hope for something else.

While it's not bad to hope for these things, the truth is that any of them are disappointing if not met, and all of them only carry temporary satisfaction. The one thing we can hope for that has lasting value is our eternity with the Lord. And that's actually exciting! Think of life without fear, pain, guilt, sorrow, sickness, loss, rejection, or death. Think about an abundance of love, joy, peace, kindness, and beauty.

When we choose to put our hope in God, we will not be disappointed. Our expectations will be *exceeded*. How often does *that* happen?

What are you currently hoping for? Can you see how hope in earthly things is only temporary? Put your hope instead in the eternal reward of living forever with Christ. How much more does that excite you?

BY FAITH
I Will Walk in Humility

*Get rid of all evil behavior. Be done with all deceit, hypocrisy, jealousy,
and all unkind speech. Like newborn babies, you must crave pure
spiritual milk so that you will grow into a full experience of salvation.
Cry out for this nourishment, now that you have had a taste
of the Lord's kindness.*

1 PETER 2:1-3, NLT

Evil behaviors are rooted in ungodly pride. When we come to faith in Jesus Christ, however, we must become like him, a humble servant, shedding our pride and living a life of honesty, integrity, contentment, and kindness. The path to this life begins with humility.

Nothing is more dependent, more completely humble, than a newborn baby. A precious life, whose only hope is a loving, kind, capable provider, lays waiting for nourishment. If placed in your arms, you alone become solely responsible for meeting her needs, even if all you can do is hand her back to her mother. But while in your arms, she humbly relies on *you* to provide.

In our spiritual infancy, we are completely humble and fully dependent on God's kindness. Our meals consist of spiritual food; putting off our old lives of sin, crying out for goodness and tasting the pure love of God. By faith, our humble path continues, though the climb gets tougher. Through it all, keep the posture of Jesus Christ your servant, who came to lose his life so you could gain the abundant, eternal, glorious life in the kingdom of heaven. By faith, walk in humility and grow in servanthood.

What behavior do you need to adjust to ensure that you are walking in humility? Submit it to the Lord and thank him for his example of servanthood.

BY FAITH
I Will Find My Inspiration in God's Word

The word of God is alive and powerful. It is sharper than the sharpest two-edged sword, cutting between soul and spirit, between joint and marrow. It exposes our innermost thoughts and desires.

HEBREWS 4:12 NLT

Have you ever opened your Bible to a random page, begun to read, and been amazed that the Scripture passage is perfectly appropriate for that exact season of your life? Then at church your pastor uses the same verse as the basis for a sermon. While driving a few days later, a worship song's lyrics match up again to your life. It's like God has a spotlight on you and is aligning the world around you to encourage, direct, or teach you wherever you are. His Word is truly *alive and powerful!*

The Word of God is a marvelously insightful gift. He gave it for our edification, education, and inspiration. Whatever we are going through, the Word of God holds the answer. Whether we are running away from God or toward him, whether we are rejoicing or mourning, however confused or secure we feel, God's Word holds the solution.

Reading his Word *exposes our innermost thoughts and desires.* Sound uncomfortable? A bit too vulnerable? We don't usually like feeling uncomfortable, and reading God's commandments brings conviction. Child of God, count this as a blessing! God shines a spotlight on these areas to inspire us toward greater submission to him. When we are submitted, we become more and more like Jesus Christ. And that is what we really want, right? By faith, find inspiration in God's Word! It is a gift, alive and powerful, to help you learn, grow, and believe.

What Scripture verses have been cropping up for you lately? Ponder those verses and their direct impact on your life today, and thank God for his living Word.

I Will Be a Woman of Integrity

Teach me your decrees, O LORD;
I will keep them to the end.
Give me understanding and I will obey your instructions;
I will put them into practice with all my heart.
Make me walk along the path of your commands,
for that is where my happiness is found.

PSALM 119:33-35 NLT

Adventurous Hollywood tales of heroes have little in common with reality, except, perhaps, the hero. Heroes really do exist. They serve us coffee, walk their dogs down our street. Maybe you are a hero. It doesn't take much really, just being in the right place at the right time. And, of course, doing the right thing. This is what sets a hero apart: a hero does the right thing.

Heroes put aside their own desires and interests. They have integrity, which means they do what most people wouldn't take the time, risk, or effort to do. David's psalm reads like an oath, a decree for heroes everywhere, spoken as a promise to uphold the integrity of God's goodness and righteousness. *Place your left hand on the Bible, raise your right hand, and repeat after me...*

How can you be a hero? How can you, by faith, be a woman of integrity? By learning God's commands and keeping them, asking for wisdom and committing to obedience, vowing devotion *with all your heart*, and submitting to walking God's path because it leads to joy. With God, you are always in the right place at the right time. By faith, a woman of integrity will do the right thing.

When was the last time you felt like you acted with integrity? How did it feel to do the right thing? Ask God for more opportunities to share his character with those around you.

BY FAITH
I Believe I Am Intimately Known by My Creator

O LORD, you have searched me and known me!
You know when I sit down and when I rise up; you discern my thoughts from afar.
You search out my path and my lying down and are acquainted with all my ways.
Even before a word is on my tongue, behold, O LORD, you know it altogether.
You hem me in, behind and before, and lay your hand upon me.
Such knowledge is too wonderful for me; it is high; I cannot attain it.
Where shall I go from your Spirit? Or where shall I flee from your presence?
If I ascend to heaven, you are there! If I make my bed in Sheol, you are there!
If I take the wings of the morning and dwell in the uttermost parts of the sea,
even there your hand shall lead me, and your right hand shall hold me.
If I say, "Surely the darkness shall cover me, and the light about me be night,"
even the darkness is not dark to you; the night is bright as the day,
for darkness is as light with you. For you formed my inward parts;
you knitted me together in my mother's womb.
I praise you, for I am fearfully and wonderfully made.
Wonderful are your works; my soul knows it very well.
My frame was not hidden from you, when I was being made in secret,
intricately woven in the depths of the earth.
Your eyes saw my unformed substance;
in your book were written, every one of them,
the days that were formed for me, when as yet there was none of them.

PSALM 139:1-16 ESV

What more confirmation is needed? By faith, hear the words of your Creator and believe: you are intimately known by him!

How do you feel when you consider that God knows every detail of your life?

I Believe That God Is Just

I will proclaim the name of the LORD; ascribe greatness to our God!
"The Rock, his work is perfect, for all his ways are justice.
A God of faithfulness and without iniquity,
just and upright is he."
DEUTERONOMY 32:3-4 ESV

Being a judge is a weighty calling; if you've ever had to judge a children's art competition, you might understand. Lovingly crafted, covered in heavy-handed brush strokes, glitter, and smiling stick figures, the smudged papers are held below smiling, expectant faces. *Which one is the best?* Could anyone choose a winner, and at the same time create a loser? More than one adult has exclaimed, "I just can't choose, they're all so wonderful!" Truly, being a judge is a calling for God alone.

Thankfully, God is great and perfect—two qualities you want in a judge. And *all his ways are justice*, he is faithful and *without iniquity*. He alone is qualified to judge mankind. He alone will bring about justice with his mighty hand, and it will be eternal. Because he is faithful and without wickedness, we can rest without worry.

Winners and losers will be declared when God comes to judge. There won't be any hesitation or argument. God has seen all the world's injustice and his judgement will be poured out. Have faith in that, but in this, as well: *his work is perfect*. His works of compassion, love, healing, and grace are perfect. And his ways of justice are perfect. This isn't true of us, but it is true of him, and he will make everything right one day. By faith, believe that God is just.

In what situations are you finding it difficult to wait for God's judgment?
Can you choose to trust that he will rule justly in his time?

BY FAITH
I Believe I Am Wholly Loved by God

Can anything ever separate us from Christ's love? Does it mean he no longer loves us if we have trouble or calamity, or are persecuted, or hungry, or destitute, or in danger, or threatened with death? (As the Scriptures say, "For your sake we are killed every day; we are being slaughtered like sheep.") No, despite all these things, overwhelming victory is ours through Christ, who loved us.

ROMANS 8:35-37 NLT

It's likely that we misunderstand, miscalculate, and misinterpret God's amazing love for us because we have nothing quite like it on earth. We get glimpses of it, and indeed we are only capable of loving by any degree because he first loved us, but nothing fully captures God's love. Nothing perfectly embodies his delight; nothing exactly mirrors his infatuation or faithfully interprets his depth of devotion. We fall remarkably short of his marvelous love.

No question, earthly love makes mistakes. Our love has limits, holds grudges, grows cold, and loses patience. Our love is blended, inextricably, with our flesh and all its capacity for sin. Human love is a faint whispered echo of the jubilant chorus of love sung out to us by God in all his parts. We can be glad he put in in written form—a love letter to his beloved—so we can carry it with us.

When you feel any shadow of a doubt about how greatly and completely God loves you, you only have to open your love letter to be reminded. You cannot be separated from this love. Unlike human love, God's has no limit, always forgives, never cools, and is steadfast. By faith, read your love letter and believe its promise: you are wholly loved by God!

What verses in the Bible remind you of God's deep love for you? Take some time to reflect on those words of love today. There is nothing that can separate you from his love.

BY FAITH
I Will Not Walk Away

"All the bridesmaids got up and prepared their lamps.
Then the five foolish ones asked the others,
'Please give us some of your oil because our lamps are going out.'
But the others replied, 'We don't have enough for all of us.
Go to a shop and buy some for yourselves.'
But while they were gone to buy oil, the bridegroom came.
Then those who were ready went in with him to the marriage feast,
and the door was locked."

MATTHEW 25:7-10 NLT

In the days leading up to Jesus' return, many believers will walk away. The ones who are unprepared for the pain, suffering, and sacrifice of those days will walk away from the truth. Their faith, under severe testing, will falter. Their lamps will go out.

This warning is for all believers. We hope that we will stand strong in the face of evil, but we cannot know how long and desperate the season of Christ's return will be. If even Peter, who walked alongside Jesus and loved him dearly, could deny him three times in one night long ago, then how can we know what we will do during the long night that is to come?

Begin filling your lamp with the oil of faith now, so that in the hour of Christ's return you will not walk away because of your emptiness. Only by faith will we make it through the night; faith is the oil that keeps the lamp lit. Our perseverance in the age of Christ's return depends on our preparation. Have you stored up enough oil for that long night? Or will you have to walk away, unprepared, before the bridegroom's return? By faith and faith alone, you will not walk away!

What does it look like for you to fill your lamp, and as many vessels as you can, with the oil of faith? Let's anticipate a long night that ends with the bridegroom's triumphant return!

BY FAITH
I Will Choose to Obey God

Now, Israel, what does the LORD your God require of you? He requires only that you fear the LORD your God, and live in a way that pleases him, and love him and serve him with all your heart and soul.

DEUTERONOMY 10:12 NLT

As Israel waits to enter the Promised Land, Moses stops beside the Jordan River. It is the last chance he will have to speak about all that the Lord commands of them. Like parents leaving a grown child at college, Moses imparts as much wisdom as possible with each word, hoping it will stay with them and guide them. It's a commencement address of sorts, spoken to a nation on the verge of independence.

His last words to his people, those he watched grow in faith and humility, are an equation for prosperity: obey God's commandments and you will be a great nation; disobey and you will be brought to destruction. Moses warns them to be careful and stay on the right path, never straying or wandering from God's commandments.

Moses repeats this simple wisdom throughout his speech, knowing better than anyone that these people are prone to distraction. They are about to enter a beautiful land, drive out its people, and take for themselves the cities, homes, fountains, fields, livestock, and vineyards within. How long will it take them to forget who it was that brought them out of slavery and into this great land?

We live amidst great distraction and temptation. God's commands are the wisdom and knowledge we need to navigate this foreign land. His commands are for our own good. By faith, choose to obey God. He will bring you into a beautiful land where you will lack nothing, and you will be thankful.

What has God asked you to obey him in recently? Can you see how important obedience is as a foundation of right living before God?

I Will Keep God as My First Love

I know you are enduring patiently and bearing up for my name's sake, and you have not grown weary. But I have this against you, that you have abandoned the love you had at first. Remember therefore from where you have fallen; repent, and do the works you did at first.

REVELATION 2:3-5 ESV

All we need is you, Lord. What can the world offer us that will not perish? What can the world give that can withstand God's refining fire? When we are tested, everything else will fall away. Only our love for him will remain. Our salvation cannot be stolen from us. God's love for us cannot be quenched. What, then, takes our eyes away from his faithful gaze?

Loving God is a *choice* we make, over and over again, because our hearts are flesh. He holds the universe and everyone on earth; we can scarcely be trusted to hold hot coffee without burning someone. We are fickle and we forget who it was that saved us, who it was that gave us a hope and a future. We have *abandoned the love we had at first.*

But it's not too late. Remember the early days of your walk with Jesus? The way your eyes were opened to understanding, how your heart was broken in love, your arms were lifted in praise, and your knees bent in repentance? God misses that. He misses the desperation you had for him, the focused time you spent in his Word, and the joy you found in prayer. His love has not diminished, and by faith, you can keep God as your first love.

Do you feel like God is still your first love? Make the choice now, and every day—every hour or minute if needed—to remember the love you had at first, and live as you did then. Abandon yourself to him because he is all you need.

BY FAITH
I Will Trust in God's Timing

*We are saved by trusting. And trusting means looking forward to getting
something we don't yet have—for a man who already has something
doesn't need to hope and trust that he will get it. But if we must keep
trusting God for something that hasn't happened yet, it teaches us to
wait patiently and confidently.*

ROMANS 8:24-25 TLB

It's hard to wait for, well, anything. We can have almost anything we want
immediately. Sometimes even waiting longer than two days to receive our order in
the mail seems way too long.

We can gain some great perspective when we think about how life was lived
hundreds or even thousands of years ago. Mail took months to travel, items were all
made-to order, and food was only delivered to your doorway if it accompanied out-
of-town guests who were planning on staying for months. We have become pretty
impatient, haven't we?

It's hard to wait for God's timing. Even when we are waiting for *good* things, we
think we shouldn't have to wait for long. Going on a missions trip, starting a job in
ministry, leading a small group, marrying the right person… doesn't God want those
things for us sooner rather than later? If we don't act now, we might miss out!

Trusting in God's timing means you believe that God won't let an opportunity
slip by unless it's not one he wants you to experience. Maybe he doesn't want it for
you now, or maybe you're not supposed to have it at all. Can you be okay with that?

*What are you waiting on God for right now? Do you trust him completely to act
at the right time?*

I Will Remain True to God Even in the Face of Persecution

If you keep quiet at a time like this, deliverance and relief for the Jews will arise from some other place, but you and your relatives will die. Who knows if perhaps you were made queen for just such a time as this?

ESTHER 4:14 NLT

Fear of man can be a paralyzing thing. *What might the cashier at the grocery store do if I dare to share the gospel as I check out?* She will probably point and shout, "This woman is a Christian! Get her!" OK, that probably wouldn't happen. Neither is the cashier likely to openly mock, jeer, or get angry and make a scene. Yet the paralyzing fear of these possibilities keeps believers from sharing the loving truth of Jesus. It's understandable, right? Can we really live a life that *desires* persecution?

Well, the answer is *yes*. Take heart! You are not alone in your fears! Esther, Queen of Persia, was also afraid to stand up for her faith. She risked death at the hand of her husband and king, and the fear paralyzed her. But she received wise counsel to speak up. She had nothing to lose and everything to gain.

Devotion to God brings persecution. When we ask Jesus to be our Savior, we recognize that only he can rescue us. The cashier cannot save, redeem, or establish our eternity. Only Jesus has done that. And the cashier doesn't have the power to take those promises away from us. The encounter with the cashier is a *"such a time as this"* moment, and we were made for these moments. By faith, remain true to God even in the face of persecution, real or perceived, and boldly proclaim the truth that saves!

How do you react in situations where you feel like you should share the Gospel with someone, but you don't know what their response will be? Ask God for the strength to remain true to him in those moments.

BY FAITH
I Will Persevere through Trials

*I eagerly expect and hope that I will in no way be ashamed, but will have
sufficient courage so that now as always Christ will be exalted in my
body, whether by life or by death.*

PHILIPPIANS 1:20, NIV

That's a pretty strong declaration: one exemplified in the life of Vibia Perpetua,
a married noblewoman and Christian martyr who died at twenty-two years of age in
Third Century Rome. There is a record of Perpetua's diary entries detailing her life in
prison and final hours. Perpetua was arrested for her profession of faith in Christ and
threatened with a harrowing execution if she did not renounce her faith. She had
many compelling reasons to do just that—a nursing infant for one!

Early martyrdom wasn't only about dying for the profession of faith. It was
about humiliation and torture carried out in a kind of sporting arena—with fans
celebrating the demise of the victims. Yet, Perpetua displayed incredible fortitude
in her final hour. Read her account and you'd have to agree that her perseverance
could not possibly have been attributed to a human characteristic.

Even with incredible dedication, endurance, and determination, we can only
hold fast for so long. Sometimes we need to recognize that it's time to call on the
supernatural strength of our Father. He gives us the perseverance to walk through
any trial.

*What are you going through today that needs a touch of supernatural
perseverance to get through? Can you be honest with God about your
need for him?*

I Will Not Be Pulled Away from God by the Temptations of this World

The LORD directs the steps of the godly.
He delights in every detail of their lives.
Though they stumble, they will never fall,
for the LORD holds them by the hand.

PSALM 37:23-24 NLT

Holding hands is beautiful when carried out in love. Two people choose to join together, leading, following, or walking as equals. We might hold hands with a child to cross the street, to help an aging stranger off the bus, or to embrace even the smallest part of our beloved while strolling through the park. We grasp hands for a moment, or many, and offer safety, kindness, or affection through the simple act.

Can you imagine God's hand extended to those who put their faith in him? Surely his sons and daughters need the spiritual comfort, guidance, and fellowship of God's hand more than any other. And we can be certain that God delights in extending his hand to us as well. The world extends an enticing but dangerous hand. It can offer comfort, guidance, and fellowship. But it can also offer anxiety, burdens, and loneliness.

Take comfort in God's kindness: he is a caring Father and he leads rightly. We cannot fall when we follow his lead because his loving grip will never let us go. As a child trusts the hand that leads them safely across the busy street, so we can trust God. By faith, you will not be pulled away from God by the temptations of the world. He is gentle, thoughtful, and compassionate, delighting over you.

Will you say "yes" to God's hand, extended gently to you? How does it make you feel, knowing that he wants to walk hand-in-hand with you through life?

BY FAITH
I Will Put On a Garment of Praise

Enter his gates with thanksgiving,
and his courts with praise.
Give thanks to him, bless his name.
For the LORD is good;
his steadfast love endures forever,
and his faithfulness to all generations.

PSALM 100:4-5 NRSV

Have you ever looked into a child's grumpy face and demanded that they don't smile? Even the most stubborn child can often be coaxed out of their funk by a few tickles or funny faces. Unfortunately, the same can't be said for adults. Imagine trying to change the attitude of a crotchety older woman with the same method. The picture is somewhat ridiculous.

When life's situations get us down, and all around us lie darkness and depression, it takes a great deal of faith to choose praise. But often that's the only thing that can really pull us out of those dark moments. When we choose to thank God for his goodness and grace, we can't help but see life in a more positive light. As we praise God, our focus shifts from ourselves to him.

God doesn't only deserve our praise when life is going well. He is worthy of our adoration every second of every day—no matter the situation. Living this out takes a good dose of faith.

What does it look like for you to put on a garment of praise today?

BY FAITH
I Believe God Hears My Prayers

In the same way the Spirit also helps our weakness; for we do not know how to pray as we should, but the Spirit Himself intercedes for us with groanings too deep for words; and He who searches the hearts knows what the mind of the Spirit is, because He intercedes for the saints according to the will of God. ROMANS 8:26-27 NASB

It is an amazing and powerful thing that the Holy Spirit within us can recognize the Holy Spirit in another believer. It unites people across geographic, economic, generational, and cultural boundaries. Two souls, surrendered to the same Savior, have plenty in common.

This miraculous connection can also bring us closer to God when we allow the Holy Spirit to show us how. When we are too weak in our flesh to know how or what to pray, we can count on the Holy Spirit to show us the way. What a relief! When the words don't seem to come out right or our supplications feel empty, we can submit to the Holy Spirit to intercede for us with prayers beyond mere words.

God hears his children. And he hears his Spirit in a language that only the holy can utter. By faith, believe that God hears your prayers. And just as two women with only Jesus in common can bond over their Messiah, the Holy Spirit in you will never run out of things to mediate to the Father. Cry out, however you can, and know that he hears every word.

What have you been wanting to tell God? Pour out your heart to him now. He is always listening.

BY FAITH
I Believe in the Protection of God

For You have been a defense for the helpless,
a defense for the needy in his distress,
a refuge from the storm, a shade from the heat.

ISAIAH 25:4 NASB

In Christ, we are protected. We have a strong shield, a faithful defender, and a constant guardian. Many have mistaken this promise as a guarantee against pain, suffering, or hardship. When sorrows overwhelm us, can we stay faithful to our protector? Will we interpret adversity as betrayal, or embrace a protection that sometimes involves endurance, anguish, and pain?

Protection does not mean perfection. Can we trust God only when our lives follow a path of ease? Faith gives depth to our expectations; we may not see through the dark clouds of the storm, but we know that God has prepared us for them. No matter how hard the rain falls or how fast the winds blow, we believe in his protection over us as we pass through it.

God's security shelters us according to what we need, not necessarily from what pains us. The storms will rage and the heat will blister, each in their turn and maybe for a long time. Can you, by faith, believe that he is protecting you through it all? His hand is upon you, defending and sheltering you; let no storm shake your faith in this, beloved.

Can you see God's hand of protection over your life even when things aren't going as you hoped? How is your faith deepened when you recognize that he is with you in the storm?

BY FAITH
I Believe God Will Provide for Me

"Ask and it will be given to you; seek and you will find; knock and the door will be opened to you. For everyone who asks receives; the one who seeks finds; and to the one who knocks, the door will be opened."

MATTHEW 7:7-8 NIV

Because of God's great and perfect knowledge of you, you can trust that he understands you, from your deepest depths to your highest heights. He knows what lies behind you and he can heal your wounds. He knows what lies ahead of you, and he can prepare you for victory. In Christ, we are given everything we need to shoulder our burdens; we are humble enough to suffer and patient enough to persevere.

He strengthens us in our season of need, not before, and sometimes the strength fades so quickly afterward that we wonder how the feat was accomplished. God asks us to press into him because much prayer is needed for the seasons to come. Gather the oil of faith now, for the days are coming when we will pour out from what we have stored up. He waits, patiently, for us to cry out for help.

God's provisions are personal to each believer. Only you can receive what he offers because you are the one knocking at his door! When he opens it, ask him what it looks like, just between the two of you, to worship? What does devotion look like? How does he want you to overcome sin? By faith, you will receive everything you need.

Why are you knocking on God's door today? What are you hoping to receive? Ask away!

BY FAITH
I Will Walk in Purity

Now that you have purified yourselves by obeying the truth so that you
have sincere love for each other, love one another deeply, from the heart.

1 PETER 1:22 NIV

Purity in Christ means rejecting judgement, bitterness, gossip, criticism, anger, selfishness, and pride, turning instead to a spotless mindset of love. Replacing the old reflex with one of love, our first reaction becomes gracious and pure. In pureness, we believe the best about one another, bear with each other's burdens, and submit to Jesus for the building up of our character.

This verse explains a process that begins when "you have purified yourselves." Purification starts with repentance from a sinful past and acceptance of salvation. You obey the truth when you put your faith and hope in God, which produces love for each other. It's an impossible gift except through Jesus, whose love is without any blemish or stain.

In contrast, we are full of stains. We judge and criticize and gossip. But with the imparting of Jesus' sincere, pure love, we can reject these habits and instead "love one another deeply, from the heart." By faith, this is how we walk in purity: loving as Christ loves and showing the compassion, understanding, encouragement, discretion, grace, patience, selflessness, and humility that is our gift through Christ.

What do you think of when you hear the word purity? Rely on Jesus to be your
character builder; then begin to love others with his love.

BY FAITH
I Believe God Has a Specific Purpose for My Life

We are God's handiwork, created in Christ Jesus to do good works,
which God prepared in advance for us to do.
EPHESIANS 2:10 NIV

Very few people know exactly what they want to be *when they grow up*. We take multiple tests to find out our personality types, strengths, and spiritual gifts, all to determine what we should do with our lives. While these tests can be good indicators of suitable opportunities, the best way to find the perfect fit is to go directly to the source.

No matter what you may have been told, you were planned by God. That means that he put you on this earth for a very specific reason. God's desire is that you will partner with him in that plan. When you begin to walk in his purpose, you will find the joy, peace, strength, and grace you need to carry it out.

Choose to believe that God has a purpose for your life, and start asking him to reveal it to you. Don't place limitations on God. He can do great things through you if you are willing to trust him.

What do you really love to do? What makes you excited about the day ahead? Do you believe God has something special for you to do? It might just be that what you're passionate about God has placed in you for a reason. Search it out!

BY FAITH
I Know God Sees Everything I Do

Let us not grow weary of doing good,
for in due season we will reap,
if we do not give up.
GALATIANS 6:9 ESV

"Look at me! Look at me! Watch this!" Oh how often children seek recognition from just about anyone who will watch. Even though the dive bomb into the water looks exactly the same as it did last time, or the cartwheel is still lopsided after thirty attempts, onlookers continue to encourage the repetitious behavior.

Are we really very different from those children? Don't we also look for recognition in life? "Look at me; I made dinner every night this week!" "See this awesome presentation I put together for work?" "You should have seen the smiles on the faces of those people I helped today." We want someone to notice our efforts, our charity, our diligence, our excellence. And, though we hate to admit it, we may even get a little upset if nobody does.

We can choose to search for recognition from others, or we can believe that God sees everything we do. Because he does. He is interested in that project we worked so hard on. He is delighted when we spend our time serving others. He loves it when we do our very best.

Don't waste your time trying to be recognized by others. Share your talents and abilities *without holding back!* Your Father in heaven has his eye on you, and he's not about to look away.

What are the things you most want God to recognize in your life?
Can you believe that he really is watching and applauding you?

BY FAITH
I Believe I Am Redeemed

"Truly, truly, I say to you, whoever hears my word and believes him who sent me has eternal life. He does not come into judgment, but has passed from death to life. Truly, truly, I say to you, an hour is coming, and is now here, when the dead will hear the voice of the Son of God, and those who hear will live."

JOHN 5:24-25 ESV

Because of Jesus Christ, we get to start over. His grace covers us and we receive his mercies anew each morning. Because of Jesus Christ, we dipped into everlasting pools of healing, baptized by the cool and refreshing presence of the Holy Spirit. We approached the throne humble, expectant, and thirsty because we could no longer shoulder the weight of our sins. Burdens unloaded at the foot of the throne; we were redeemed for freedom and live now in the promise of life everlasting. We have *passed from death to life.*

We have the assurance of our redemption, but do we live like the redeemed every day? Do we rejoice like slaves who have been set free? Redeemed, we abandon the path once walked for the one navigated by God. Slaves cannot determine their steps; they are ordered to walk. But children of God have been ransomed and set free. They must choose to run from the paths of materialism, pride, vanity, and idolatry that have been paved by the world.

Being redeemed means being reinvented, refurbished, and revitalized. Something broken, ugly, or useless is given purpose. We are given a purpose in our redemption: to plead with those still in bondage to break free from their chains. The hour is coming when it will be too late.

Spend some time expressing your thanks to God for the redemptive work of his Son in your life. Believe that he has truly erased every sin you have confessed.

BY FAITH
I Will Rest in God When I Need to Be Refreshed

Bless the LORD, O my soul, and forget not all his benefits,
who forgives all your iniquity, who heals all your diseases,
who redeems your life from the pit,
who crowns you with steadfast love and mercy,
who satisfies you with good
so that your youth is renewed like the eagle's.

PSALM 103:2-5 ESV

Is it reasonable to believe that a marathon runner can finish a race without a single refreshing cup of water? Would it be fair to expect a doctor, after working a 36-hour shift, to have the energy to perform one last tedious surgery? Can a child be expected not to lick the spatula that mixed the cookie dough? Or should a foreigner be intuitively familiar with the customs of a new land?

We know that humans have limits. We need to eat and drink regularly. We get tired and struggle if we don't have enough sleep. We learn patience and self-control as we get older, but our emotions can be overwhelmed by life's great upheavals. The shepherd king David knew this, and understood God's gracious and loving path of refreshment.

Whether you are at peak performance or running on empty, needing renewal now or in the future, God alone can give you what you need for the refreshment of your mind, body, and spirit because he knows your limits and capabilities. He knows that you need time to refuel, space to recover your strength, and that sometimes a little cookie dough goes a long way.

By Faith, rest in God when you need to be refreshed. Don't believe that you aren't strong because you need to rest; you aren't meant be strong forever. You are designed to lean on the one whose strength can renew you.

What do you need your strength renewed for today? Can you train yourself to believe that God wants you to ask him for rest and refreshment—every time you need it?

I Will Contend for Peace in My Relationships

Don't just pretend to love others. Really love them. Hate what is wrong. Hold tightly to what is good. Love each other with genuine affection, and take delight in honoring each other. Do all that you can to live in peace with everyone.

ROMANS 12:9-10, 18 NLT

These are very convicting directions from God's Word. Unless you have completely mastered loving everyone you meet, Paul's words to the Roman church might leave you feeling a little squeamish. How can we determine to *really love* each other? In the same breath we can *hate* what is wrong and then *do* what is wrong. We are holding tightly to what is good, but at the smallest distraction we let go and grab hold of something shinier. Someone we genuinely love and delight to honor can become an easy target for our criticism and jealousy.

We are flawed. Deeply and truly we are flawed, but not hopelessly. If God commands that we *do all that we can to live at peace with everyone*, we can believe that he has made a way for us to achieve it. Begin with confession and repentance. Cry out to God for his Holy Spirit to change you from the inside—your thoughts, your opinions, your outlook—so that your words and deeds will also be transformed.

Ask for God's love for others to overwhelm your heart so you can *really love them*. Ask for his mindset to replace yours, and cling tightly to his good Word. Read it and meditate on it, day and night, so that it is painted on the walls of your mind. By faith, contend for peace in all relationships by putting off old habits and adopting God's heart of love.

Which relationships in your life need peace right now? Ask God to give you his heart of love and forgiveness toward those people today.

BY FAITH
I Believe God Will Not Disappoint Me

Those who love me, I will deliver;
I will protect those who know my name.
When they call to me, I will answer them;
I will be with them in trouble,
I will rescue them and honor them.

PSALM 91:14-15 NRSV

There's something to be said for a reliable car. It starts *every* time you turn the key over. It *never* breaks down and leaves you stranded in the middle of a highway. It *always* blows heat in the cold of winter and cold air in the heat of summer.

If we want our cars to be reliable, we want people to be even more so. They *always* show up when they say they will. They *never* forget to finish their part of an important project. *Every* time you call, they pick up the phone.

We all know that neither cars nor people are completely reliable. What we do know is that both cars and people will fail us at some point in our lives. It's inevitable. Aren't you glad to be in relationship with someone who cannot fail you because it is not in his nature to fail—*ever*? Our perfect God is always near. He doesn't forget about our important plans or our hopes and dreams. He won't be caught off guard when it's our birthday, anniversary, graduation day, important final interview, or anything in between.

God wants what is best for us and he has the means to see it happen. What are you hoping for from him today? You can be sure that when you place your focus on the Lord, you will not be disappointed.

BY FAITH
I Will Not Let Others' Opinions of Me Matter More than God's

Let all that I am praise the LORD;
may I never forget the good things he does for me.
He forgives all my sins
and heals all my diseases.
He redeems me from death
and crowns me with love and tender mercies.
He fills my life with good things.
My youth is renewed like the eagle's!

PSALM 103:2-5, NLT

God created you for relationship with him, just as he created Adam and Eve. He delights in your voice, your laughter, and your ideas. He longs to fellowship with you just as he did with his first son and daughter. But, like Adam and Eve, we are sometimes persuaded by the opinions of others instead of listening and obeying the commands of our Father and greatest friend.

It is understandably tempting to share our grievances, triumphs, problems, or desires with friends and loved ones we can easily call on the phone or meet for coffee. God has given us wonderful relationships! But we run the risk of listening first to their opinions rather than God's, and this risk can trap us in sin.

When life gets difficult, we can run to him with our frustrations. When we're overwhelmed with sadness or grief, we can carry our pain to him. In the heat of anger or frustration, we can call on him for freedom. He is a friend that offers all of this—and more—in mercy and love, and he is worthy of our friendship.

By Faith, do not let others' opinions of you matter more than God's. Train your heart to run first to God with your pain, joy, frustration, and excitement. His friendship will never let you down!

How much value do you place on the opinions of others? Do you know how much God loves you and wants to share in your everyday moments?

I Will Develop Maturity in My Walk with God

We know how much God loves us, and we have put our trust in his love.
God is love, and all who live in love live in God, and God lives in them.
And as we live in God, our love grows more perfect. So we will not be
afraid on the day of judgment, but we can face him with confidence
because we live like Jesus here in this world.

1 JOHN 4:16 NLT

Responsibility is something that is sorely lacking in the world. We have excuses for everything. We even have excuses for excuses. Nothing is anyone's fault, and we are encouraged to live solely for ourselves.

Without responsibility, how can we expect to grow in our relationship with God? We can't live oblivious to our fault or the needs around us. God calls us to a higher level of living. He asks us to love him first and our neighbor next. He tells us to respect each other, to consider others as more important than ourselves. It's so counter-culture that we have to really work at developing it.

But as we do, we recognize his heart for others and we begin to carry compassion and a desire to help. As we love God, we gain better understanding of his love for us, and we become more aware of our need for his grace. This is the maturity that he desires for us: closeness to him, and relationship with others.

What areas in your life are lacking a sense of responsibility? Ask the Lord to give you his heart, and watch as you become more aware of his maturing work in your life.

BY FAITH
I Know God Will Lift Me Up
when I Fall

You, O Lord, are a shield about me,
My glory, and the One who lifts my head.
PSALM 3:3, NASB

Picture a young girl running a race. She leaps off to a great start when the gun sounds. She pushes her way to the front of the pack in no time and sets a pace that is tough to compete with. As she rounds the final corner with the finish line in sight, she stumbles. She tries desperately to regain her balance, but it's too late. She crashes to the ground. Trying to be brave, she jumps up and sprints the final yards to complete the race. Fourth place.

Head hung low, skinned knees burning, and vision blurry, she walks over to her coach. He gently lifts her chin to the sun, and brushes away the tears that have spilled over. As her bottom lip begins to quiver, he reassures her that everything is going to be okay. That life is full of painful moments that creep up unexpectedly, but it's also full of second chances. "Don't give up on yourself," he says, "I haven't given up on you."

When we've given up, run away, lost the plot, or stumbled and fallen, God doesn't give up on us. When we come to him with our heads hung low, he lifts our chins, looks deep into our eyes, and whispers tender words of compassion that reach the deepest places in our hearts.

Do you feel like you can't look up? How do you think God feels about you in this moment? Let your face be tipped to the Son. Allow the words of Jesus to wash over your wounds and bring healing to your heart, soul, and mind today.

I Will Seek After That Which Brings Eternal Reward

"Don't store up treasures here on earth, where moths eat them and rust destroys them, and where thieves break in and steal. Store your treasures in heaven, where moths and rust cannot destroy, and thieves do not break in and steal. Wherever your treasure is, there the desires of your heart will also be."

MATTHEW 6:19-21 NLT

There are many so-called *experts* ready and willing to give you advice (usually for a price) about any problem you have. Whether you are dealing with health issues, money matters, relationship woes, career dilemmas, car troubles, housing hassles, or pet problems, there is an expert out there ready to diagnose and treat it. If you lived in the neighborhood of Galilee two-thousand years ago, you would've had access to the world's greatest advisor. His advice was free... sort of.

Jesus asked that you be willing to give up everything you had to follow him. Your job, your family, your house and wealth—all were given up for the sake of following Jesus the Messiah. If he were advising you today, would you listen? In Matthew 6, Jesus teaches us to forsake all earthly gain because it is temporary and vulnerable. Real treasures, he instructed, should be stored in heaven where they will be safe.

Eternal treasures are a reward worth seeking, and Jesus' instructions are advice worth taking. When we pray quietly, for God's ears only, he hears and will reward us. When we give to the needy in private, without telling others about it, God sees our sacrifice and will reward us. The praise and approval of the world is fleeting and worthless compared to the treasure that God stores up for us as we forsake earthly gain. Take Jesus' perfect advice and, by faith, seek after that which brings eternal reward.

Evaluate the things you spend your time on. What has eternal reward attached to it?

I Place My Security in God

Whom have I in heaven but you?
And earth has nothing I desire besides you.
My flesh and my heart may fail,
but God is the strength of my heart
and my portion forever.
PSALM 74:25-26 NIV

When considering a home remodeling project, it's important to determine where the support beams are. If we just knock a wall down here and there to create more space, it could have a detrimental effect on the rest of the structure. In fact, it could even lead to irreparable damage. Whether a building topples because of faulty construction, a bad foundation, or extraordinary loads, you can bet the support beams were compromised.

Support beams can be like those people in our lives that we look up to. People we love. People we respect. People we depend on. People we find our security in. Sometimes they fall—and we might not realize we were leaning on them until they do. When they go down, it can be hard to recover. They might leave a wake of destruction in their collapse.

The only support beam you can lean on and guarantee it will never shake, bend, or crumble under pressure is God. When the world around you seems to have collapsed, and you find yourself floundering around looking for something firm to take hold of, grab God's hand. He is steady and secure.

What support beams have you experienced tumbling down around you?
Do you know how much the Lord desires to be your security when everything else
crumbles? Ask him to hold you up today. He is more than capable of bearing
your load.

I Will Take Hold of the Promises of God and I Won't Let Go

Understand, therefore, that the LORD your God is indeed God.
He is the faithful God who keeps his covenant for a thousand
generations and lavishes his unfailing love on those who love him
and obey his commands.

DEUTERONOMY 7:9 NLT

His promises are so good! Is there one that is better than another? He promises to protect, heal, comfort, love, forgive, provide, equip, overcome, abide, listen, delight, guide, fulfill, understand, reward, renew, refresh, bless, lead, redeem… the list goes on longer than these pages. But promises get made and broken every day. How can we trust that God's promises are true?

God has been faithful to his covenants since he promised Adam and Eve that nothing good would come from eating the fruit of that tree. He continues his faithfulness to you, his daughter and his delight. All of his promises are as true for you as they were for Noah, Abraham, Joseph, and David. He can rescue you from disaster, make you flourish in the wilderness, redeem you from despair, and knit your heart together with his in deep friendship and devotion. *If you will only believe.*

When we understand that he is, indeed, the God of the universe and of our hearts, we cannot help but fall to our knees. When we give him the honor and glory that he is owed, when the greatness of his name and the power of his love overwhelm us, we are undone. Falling under the weight of our own sin, our posture is humbled to the one who overcame sin for our sake. We can only respond with love and obedience to such a king.

Don't ever let go of his promises. By faith, take hold of them and overcome!

Are you struggling to believe that his promises are for you? Take some time to sit in his presence and dwell on his goodness. Tell him how much you want to believe that his promises are true.

I Believe That God Knows What Is Best for Me

What a God you are! Your path for me has been perfect!
All your promises have proven true.
What a secure shelter for all those
who turn to hide themselves in you!
You are the wrap-around God giving grace to me.
PSALM 18:30 TPT

Why don't parents let their children eat candy for breakfast, lunch, and dinner? The answer is obvious. It wouldn't be *good* for them. But ask the children what they think, and they could probably come up with a pretty convincing argument that candy *is* good for them.

In life, situations come along that seem good. We think that man would make the perfect husband, or that job would be the best jumpstart to our career, or that adventure would be the ultimate experience. The problem is we don't have the vantage point that God does. All those opportunities might be "candy," and what we really need is a good, nutritious meal.

When we let go of the idea that we know what's best, and choose to believe that God actually does, we will find what is truly good. How wonderful it is to know that we don't have to feel the pressure of making all the right choices on our own.

What experiences in your life seemed good, but turned out being less than God's best for you? God has this amazing way of nurturing us even when we choose to eat candy. We just have to admit that his way would have been better and move forward in his grace.

BY FAITH
I Will Stand on the Truth of God's Word

The sum total of all your words adds up to absolute truth,
and every one of your righteous decrees is everlasting.
Your promises are the source of my bubbling joy;
the revelation of your Word thrills me
like one who has discovered hidden treasure.

PSALM 119:160, 162 TPT

The world shouts, "Truth is relative!" "Truth is what I believe!" "Truth is what I want it to be!" We cannot entertain these lies. Truth is found in God's Word alone. Truth is absolute. It has not changed since the beginning of time and it will not change on into eternity.

Because God's Word is true, we can believe everything it says. It's by far not the most popular thing to stake our morals, beliefs, and decisions on, and we can be sure to expect a good amount of opposition and ridicule when we do. This is why it's important to surround ourselves with others who also believe wholeheartedly in the absolute nature of God's Word. Stand together in faith and declare that God's Word is the definition of truth itself.

What does it look like for you to stand on the truth of God's Word in this season of your life?

BY FAITH
I Know That God Truly Understands My Heart

*Jesus… understands our weaknesses, for he faced all of the same
testings we do, yet he did not sin. So let us come boldly to the throne of
our gracious God. There we will receive his mercy, and we will find grace
to help us when we need it most.*

HEBREWS 4:15-16 NLT

My Daughter,
Don't lose heart. Guard your faith and listen to my voice. I understand your
love for me. You may think it's small or diminishing, but I feel its strength and
fullness. You love like a child—believing and carefree. Keep your eyes fixed on me,
beloved. I understand your needs. I am a refuge and strength for you; only I can
and will sustain you. My care is what is right for you: I am your stream of water, your
living sacrifice, your good shepherd. I am your comfort and my mercy is complete.
I understand your heart and all its pains, sorrows, longings, and disappointments,
and I comfort you. I never leave you or forsake you. I love you so much.

Whatever you need, you can ask him and he will answer you; he already knows
your heart and what you long for. Nothing is a surprise to him! By faith, know that
God truly understands your heart. He knows the test you are facing, and he gives
you the mercy you need to endure it. *When you need it most,* his grace is there.

*Write a letter back to God, expressing your gratitude for his deep
understanding of your heart.*

I Trust God to Give Me Wisdom in Every Situation

*Then you will understand what is right, just, and fair,
and you will find the right way to go.
For wisdom will enter your heart,
and knowledge will fill you with joy.
Wise choices will watch over you.
Understanding will keep you safe.*

PROVERBS 2:9-11 NLT

All of life is a test. As we live each day, the tests we face teach us valuable lessons. It may seem backwards: usually lessons are learned to prepare us for a test. But in life, the test often comes first. Through the lessons, God gives us the wisdom we need for the next test.

It's a safe bet that the tests will keep coming, right? Thankfully, our hearts gain understanding every time. Tension and uncertainty melt away; joy blossoms. Solomon's advice is that we listen to wisdom, apply it, and learn as we go. Then we will have understanding; we will find the right path with wisdom in our hearts and joy from knowledge. We will be safe. *Yes, please.*

Gaining wisdom doesn't guarantee that you won't stumble and fall on your face or stick your foot in your mouth. You will still make mistakes, say the wrong thing at the wrong time, and wish you could go back in time and do it right. It stings. But even when we fail the test, we learn a lesson and gain wisdom... if we humble ourselves. By faith, we can trust that God will give us wisdom in every situation. Another test is just around the corner, waiting for you to pass with flying colors!

What valuable lessons have you learned from life's tests? Take joy in the wisdom you gain from those tests. Thank God for giving you the opportunity to make wise choices.